SNEAKER
RESTORATION GUIDE

BY JAYLEN BOYD

Copyright © 2016 Anaghe Inc
All rights reserved.
ISBN:

YOUR MEMBERSHIP AT WWW.ANAGHE.COM IS FREE WITH THE PURCHASE OF THIS BOOK TO REDEEM YOUR MEMBERSHIP&WATCH THE INSTRUCTIONAL VIDEOS PLEASE FOLLOW THE STEPS BELOW.

BOOK BUYERS : SIGN UP ON THE WEBSITE AND FORWARD PROOF OF PURCHASE (RECEIPT WITH CONFIRMATION #)AN APPROVAL NOTIFACATION WILL BE SENT BY EMAIL WITH IN 24 HRS.

NEW MEMBERS : MAKE MEMBERSHIP PAYMENT FOR EBOOK DOWNLOAD &

VIDEO ACCESS THEN SIGN UP ON THE SITE FOR YOUR APPROVAL NOTIFACATION ALLOW UP TO 24 HRS FOR PROCESSING.

SNEAKER RESTORATION GUIDE

BY JAYLEN BOYD
Copyright

2016 by

Anaghe Inc.

All rights reserved. Written permission must be secured from the publisher to use or reproduce any part of this book, except for brief quotations in critical reviews or articles.

WWW.ANAGHE.COM

https://www.youtube.com/user/AnagheInc

Table of Contents

Introductions 6

Chapter One: Clean 7

Chapter Two: Crease Treatment 13

Chapter Three: Oxidation 17

Chapter Four: Paint 20

Chapter Five: Detailing 24

Conclusion 30

Applied Techniques 31

Introductions

We at Anaghe Inc. pride ourselves in producing quality professional craftsmanship in our sewn products. Whether it's building a clothing line from scratch or cleaning your favorite pair of kicks. There is an order of steps that need to be established to truly receive the best results possible. This instructional book is the most in depth sneaker restoration manual on the market today, also the only one of its kind. It's made with video, plus detailed pictures to give the reader/viewer as much guidance as they need to successfully complete a full restoration. If you have no experience, want to save a few bucks or have been bringing shoes back to life for years I'm positive this book has tricks and tips to help elevate your game. Every tool mentioned in the steps are HOUSEHOLD PRODUCTS, that can be obtained by any able person. It also helps simplify things rather than showing processes with dangerous chemicals that the any person can't obtain or use properly. That route is expensive and there is no reason to over complicate things. Never the less "The Sneaker Restoration Guide Vol. 1" will be a great money saving buy for whom whoever uses its riches.

Chapter One: Clean

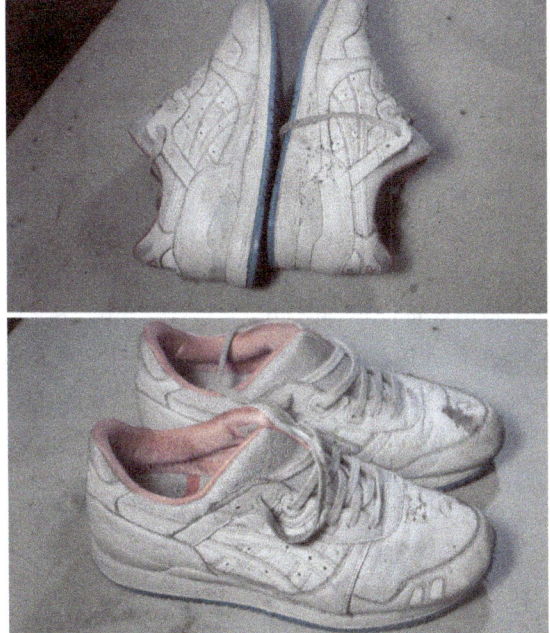

The true first thing to do is placing the shoes on the table aka work surface and remove the laces

SNEAKER RESTORATION GUIDE

Afterwards the insoles should be removed if called for. Next, we must stuff the shoes to give them shape, make them easier to work with, and bulge the creases out. Bulging the creases is needed for later processes. Proper preparations prevent poor quality. You're probably asking yourself what do I stuf the shoes with. There are a wide range of "fillers" to use. These include pillowcases, towels, washcloths, old t-shirt, ect. Basically whatever you can fit inside the shoe that is flexible, and will give it a fresh out the box appearance.

Now we move to what we be using to clean the sneakers. A mix of any household dish soap with a few drops of acetone/nail polish remover (If needed) will service. Mix two cups one will be the cup that you soak your laces in.

Using one cup is a bad idea because your laces may not get as clean. Also you may be required to change the solution into the shoe cleaning cup depending on how bad the job is, can usually tell before you actually do anything. As for the brush used any household appropriate sized cleaning brush will be perfect. Some people prefer an old tooth brush for the fact that you can hit small spaces and its less abrasive then bigger brushes. Any brush is fine really. Just as a reminding keep a towel at your work station for spills and to check the work.

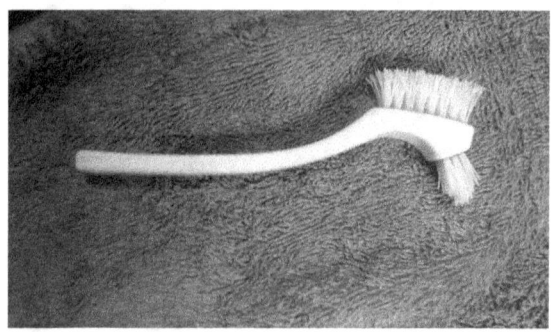

Finally ready to clean them. Take your toothbrush dip it in the soapy water and scrub gently. Wipe away soap and dirty after scrubbing the whole shoe then check work. It's easier this way rather than wiping dirt away after every panel. Repeat this until entire shoe is finished. Make sure to clean every surface behind tab, lining, everything. Even the bottom of the shoes...if you want, just do that last.

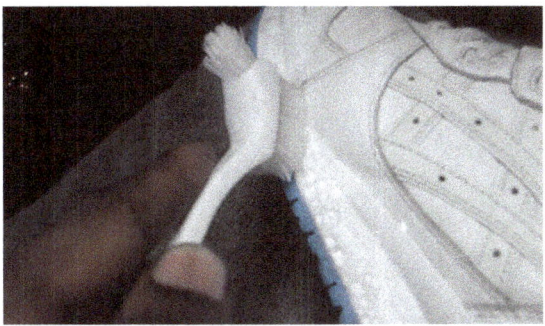

After going back over all the trouble areas making sure nothings missed or underworked on. Anyway of course we want the dirt gone but a key purpose of the clean phases is to show you how much more work the show needs. These include oxidation, creases, scraped leather or paint, and scuffs. The issues describe will be addressed later on. If these things are treated in any order work will have to be gone over again and again, Its best to do everything just once without confusion, simply, and smooth.

SNEAKER RESTORATION GUIDE

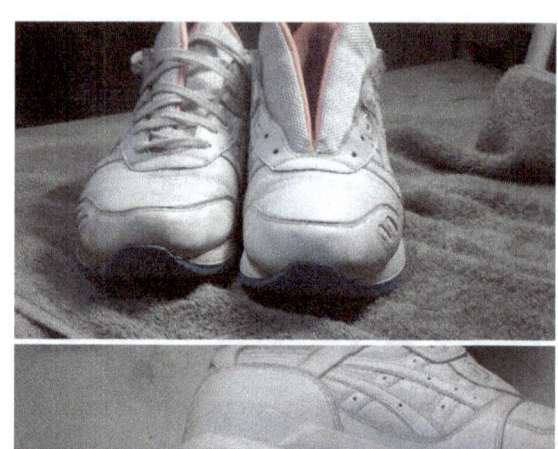

Chapter Two:
Crease Treatment

      The logical second step in this restoration is to pull the creases out of the shoes. First you must plug in your iron and set it to wool. For a hot but not hot enough to burn the material on the toe box. Make sure the steam setting is on high. The steam plays a big part because it stretches and straightens the material. Place a semi-damp towel over the toe box and run the iron over the creased areas. There should be no direct contact between the sneaker and the iron.

SNEAKER RESTORATION GUIDE

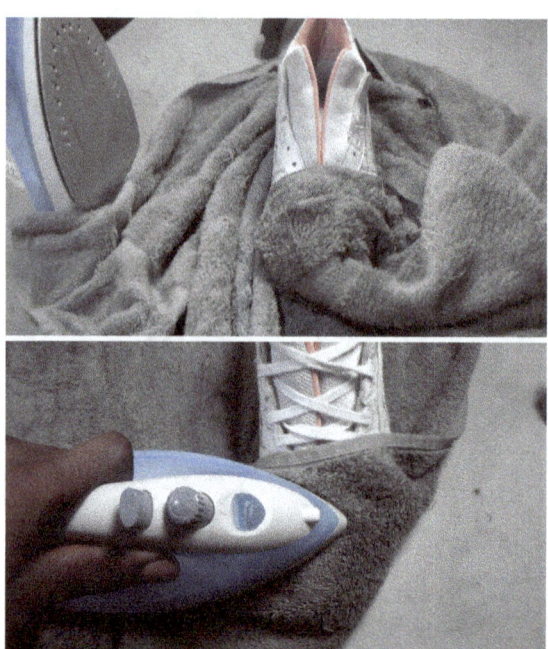

Afterwards, let the shoes sit in the steam with the towel still on them. Let them cool down before checking the work. To correct any deep creases simply shape the shoe how you wish and stuff the area further. Creases should gradually fade away. So keep repeating the process till you receive the desired effect. Now there is another part of the shoe that usually requires this and it's the sole.

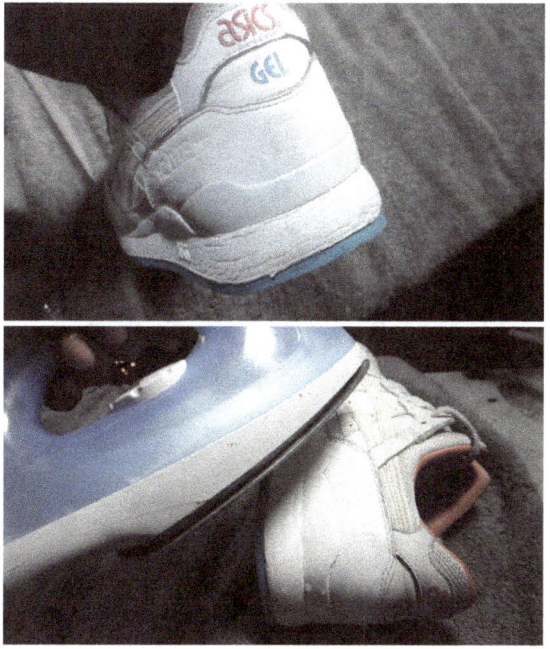

The process should be used the same way in this area. The difference handling this portion is the iron should NEVER touch the shoe and you don't have to use the towel; the steam will do all the work.

SNEAKER RESTORATION GUIDE

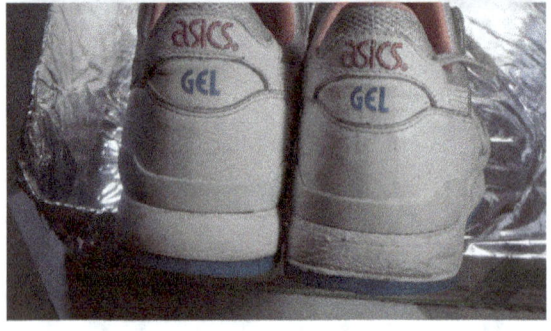

Chapter Three: Oxidation

Oxidation occurs on the light colored or clear, plastics, and rubber bottoms of the shoe. This is cause by the long term exposure to the sun and air. The first thing we need to do is take your cleaning brush and salon care 40 plus.

Salon Care is the product that reverses oxidation. Now take your brush and dip it in the salon care, be liberal and scrub it to oxidized parts.

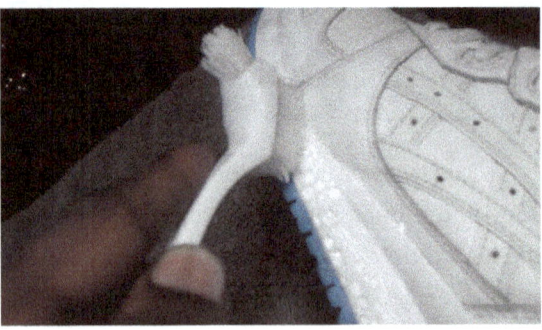

Cover with cling wrap to keep the conditioner from drying out.

Place the shoe in direct sunlight for 2-4 hour sessions. Check periodically to make sure the conditioner has not dried out and that there is no damage to the soles. Like the crease treatment it will be gradual so repeat the process until desired finish is reached. WARNING this might take awhile. Also if you mark the shoe or it doesn't go right in the process no fear it will be addressed in the detailing portion. One last thing if anyone is wondering, yes you can use artificial lights for this, but sunlight is accessible to everyone in any household so it won't be touched on in this guide. The last thing to do in this step is cleaning off the salon care and taping for paint.

Chapter Four: Paint

This is one of the most important portions of the restoration process. Well they're all important but after repainting the grip the difference jumps out at you. In the last selection we left off at taping so we'll start there.

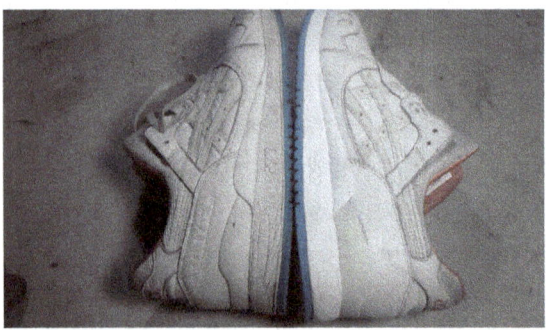

Remember what I said about mishaps. When in the oxidation process there was discoloring caused by too long exposure or not enough conditioner..

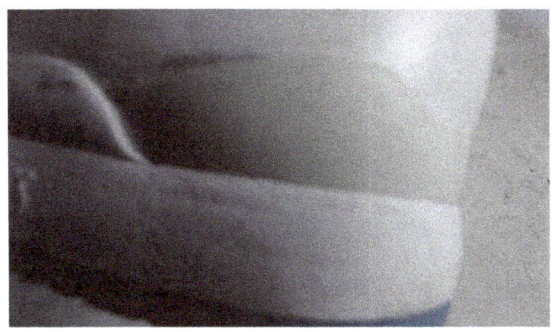

Any way it goes now I can show you how to fix it. Taping and the prep process before actually laying paint is the key to a clean efficient job. The type of paint and finish you use doesn't matter as long as they are acrylic but it should match the original. I use synthetic brushes because they don't leave bristles, streaks or loose shape easily

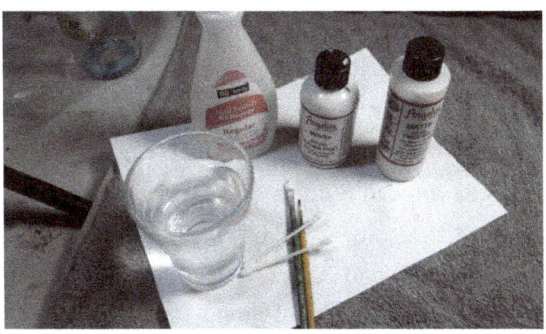

The first thing to do is to tape off everything but the parts being painted. Grab a clean sharp razor and cut out exact lines. Take your time, the more careful you are the more accurate and clean the work will be. Take some acetone (nail polish remover) and a q-tip and clean the top layers of finish and paint off. Next take your paint brush, dip it in the paint and apply your first layer. Brush strokes should be horizontal and in one direction. After finishing a layer take a blow dryer, at a good distance dry the paint out. It makes the paint into a durable shell along with making everything quicker. The faster one layer dries the quicker you can put the next layer on. Keep adding layers until the color is solid. This is usually after 4-5 coats. After this is all complete remove all tape, add a thin layer of finisher to seal the work and you are finished ready for the last step.

JAYLEN BOYD

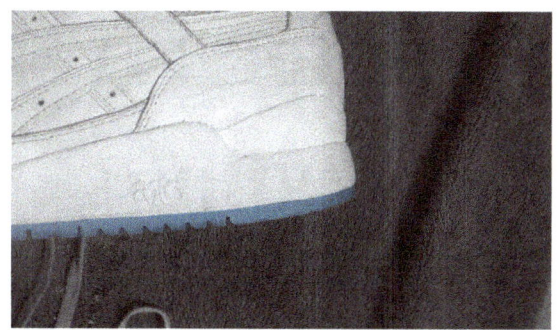

SNEAKER RESTORATION GUIDE

Chapter Five: Detailing

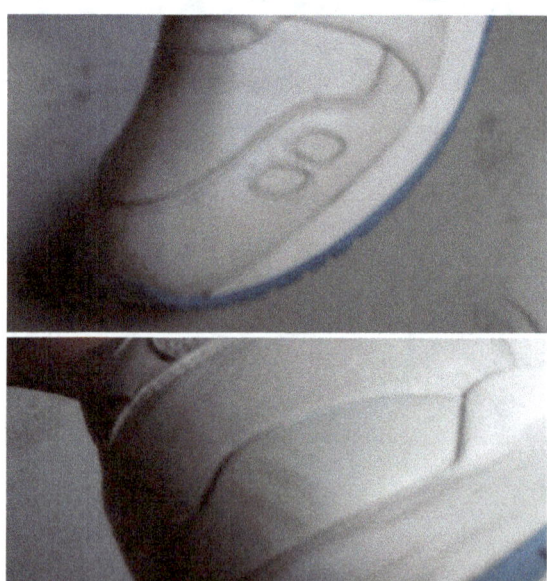

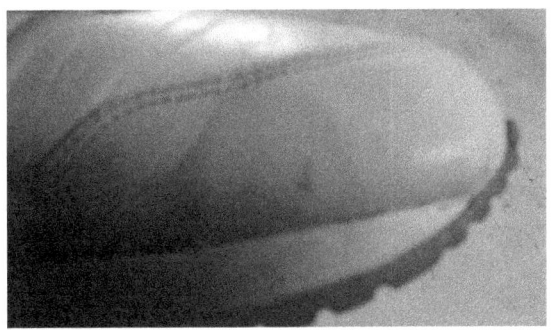

For this part is the fine tuning the sneaker and controlling the quality. First remove scuffs with a q-tip dipped in acetone.

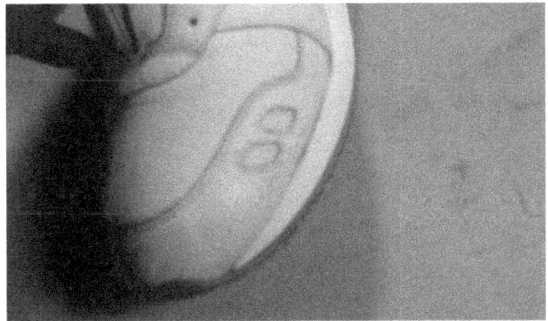

SNEAKER RESTORATION GUIDE

There is not a lot of acetone needed. After scrub the shoes again for a final clean. Next paint over the ripped patches, and bare spots on the shoes with the smallest brush you can find.

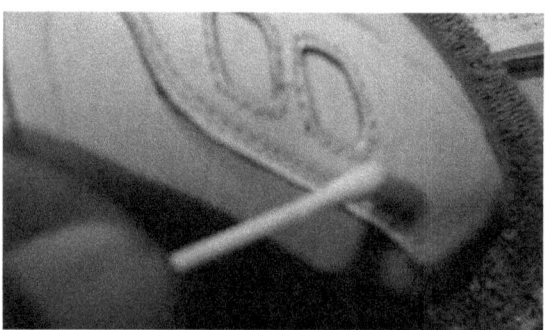

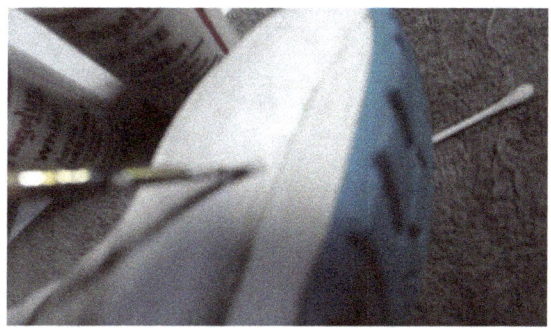

Add a little finisher to the spots and dry them to lock in the work.

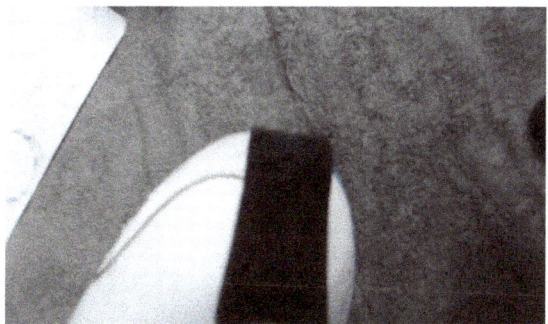

Once that is done remove fillers and put the laces back in. The restoration is complete and your brand new sneakers are ready for wear or storage.

SNEAKER RESTORATION GUIDE

JAYLEN BOYD

Conclusion

There are many reasons we restore sneakers. Some do it for profit, other because they love their shoes, others just don't want to spend money all the time for brand new sneakers. Well in any case we all love sneakers and restoring classics and being able to personalize what you have keeps our culture thriving. Restorations for sneakers are like those for cars. Those old beaters you junked could have been worth something one day.

JAYLEN BOYD

Applied Techniques

SNEAKER RESTORATION GUIDE

These KD's had paint loss and scuffs on the inner heels and toebox . Following the same steps listed in this manual and paint mixing methods to develop certain colors. You can bring any pair of sneakers back to life.

SNEAKER RESTORATION GUIDE

BEFORE

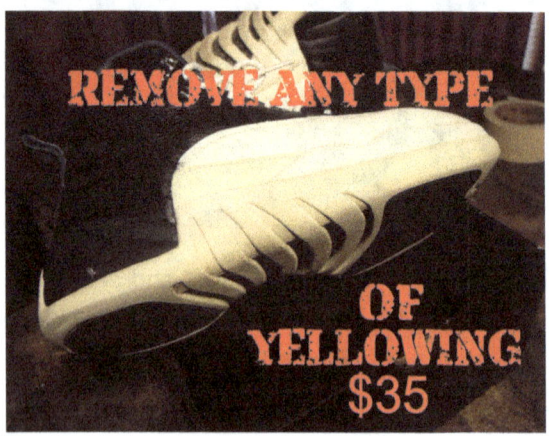

AFTER

The bottoms of these 2s were oxidized but sauce and the sun cleared the yellow away.

BEFORE

JAYLEN BOYD

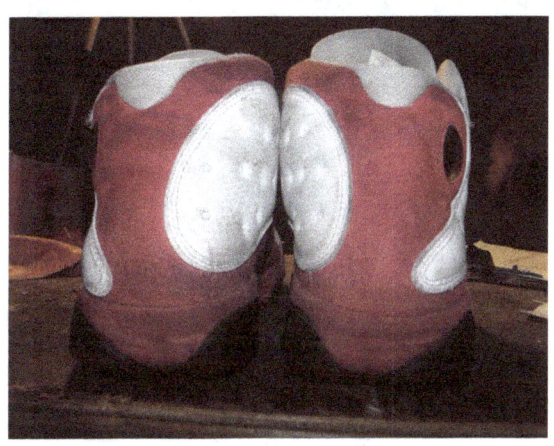

SNEAKER RESTORATION GUIDE

AFTER

These 13s have had a full restoration along with suede dying.

BEFORE

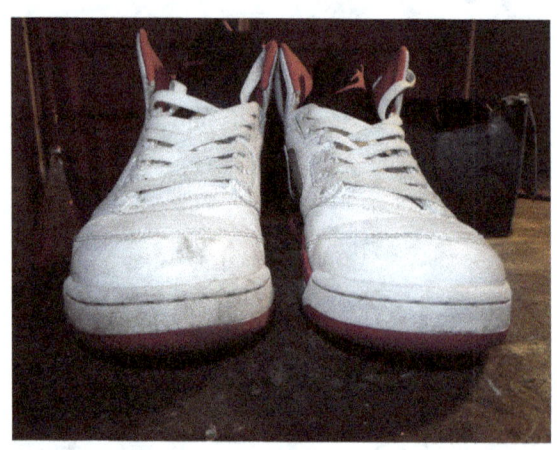

AFTER

Cleaned, scuffs removed and repainted for a perfect finish.

BEFORE

JAYLEN BOYD

SNEAKER RESTORATION GUIDE

AFTER

JAYLEN BOYD

www.ingramcontent.com/pod-product-compliance
Lightning Source LLC
Chambersburg PA
CBHW070553300426
44113CB00011B/1899